DO NOT DISTURB

by

Billy Van Zandt
&
Jane Milmore

SAMUEL FRENCH, INC.

45 West 25th Street   NEW YORK 10010
7623 Sunset Boulevard HOLLYWOOD 90046
LONDON   TORONTO

IMPORTANT BILLING AND CREDIT REQUIREMENTS

All producers of DO NOT DISTURB *must* give credit to the Authors of the Play in all programs distributed in connection with performances of the Play and in all instances in which the title of the Play appears for purposes of advertising, publicizing or otherwise exploiting the Play and/or a production. The names of the Authors *must* also appear on a separate line, on which no other name appears, immediately following the title, and *must* appear in size of type not less than fifty percent the size of the title type.

Do Not Disturb opened at the Henderson Theatre, Lincroft, New Jersey, Friday, May 24, 1991.

The Cast
(In Order of Appearance)

ACT I
SCENE 1
"The Pick-Up"

Melissa	Jane Milmore
Ken	Glenn Jones
Carl	Billy Van Zandt

SCENE 2
"The Superstar"

Jack	Glenn Jones
Annie	Sherle Tallent

SCENE 3
"The Blue Movie"

Bellhop	Billy Van Zandt
Erikka	Sally Vold Winters
Cubby	Drew Hollywood
Lyle	Glenn Jones

ACT II
SCENE 1
"The Wedding"

Glenn.. Glenn Jones
Walter .... Billy Van Zandt
Claudia............................ Sally Vold Winters
Mrs. Kirschenbaum...................Sherle Tallent
Wendy ....Jane Milmore
Rabbi Huchelman.................. Drew Hollywood

SCENE 2
"The Rendezvous"

Sheila...................................Jane Milmore
Craig .... Billy Van Zandt
Loretta.......................... Sally Vold Winters

SCENE 3
"The Final Exit"

Man................................. Billy Van Zandt

Produced by Mark Fleming
Directed by Mr. Van Zandt
Set Design: Chad Heulitt
Lighting Design: Joseph Rembisz
Costume Design: Kitty Cleary
Stage Manager: Neil Murphy
Sound Design: Jane Milmore

ACT I

SCENE 1
"The Pick-up"

SCENE: A plush New York City hotel room.
Center stage is a king-sized bed and two night tables.
Stage right is the suite's main door, which opens into the
room. Next to it is a desk, telephone and chair. Upstage
of the front door is an adjoining room door, which is
closed.
Upstage left is an archway that leads off to the bathroom
and a door-less closet rack.
Stage left sit a table and two chairs, and the television—all
of which are in front of a picture window through which
we see a New York city night-time skyline.

AT RISE: The scene opens on an empty hotel room. The
door opens and a BUSINESSMAN enters with a
beautiful young LADY. SHE is a true free spirit and
it's obvious he just picked her up downstairs. THEY
kiss and attack each other as they enter.

KEN. Oh, Melissa.
MELISSA. Oh, Ken.
KEN. I want you.
MELISSA. And I want you.
KEN. I want you more.
MELISSA. Yes, you probably do.

KEN. Melissa, I don't know what it is about you. But the second our eyes met tonight, I've felt I've known you my entire life.

MELISSA. That's how I feel too. Oh, boy, this is so neat.

KEN. I didn't think I would ever find someone like you.

MELISSA. Here I am.

KEN. There you are.

MELISSA. Are you sure you're not married?

KEN. Of course not.

MELISSA. Promise?

KEN. Of course I promise.

(As THEY continue to kiss necks and cheeks.)

MELISSA. No girlfriend?

KEN. Nobody. I broke up with my last girlfriend six months and fourteen days ago. There's been no one since then that's interested me, but tonight ... I saw you ... and pow. I can't believe we're here.

MELISSA. It must be fate. You're the first guy I've really wanted to be with since my boyfriend and I broke up too.

KEN. Really?

MELISSA. Oh, yes. And I do really want to be with you.

KEN. And I really want to be with you.

MELISSA. You told me.

KEN. I know. Champagne?

MELISSA. Sure.

(SHE starts bouncing on the bed.)

MELISSA. But I don't know if I should. Champagne makes me lose my inhibitions.

KEN. Inhibitions?

MELISSA. (*Does somersaults on the bed.*) Things might get really, really wild. Maybe you're not ready for that yet.

KEN. (*Watching her body roll around.*) I'm ready. I'm ready. Oh God, am I ready.

MELISSA. Are you sure?

(*SHE bounces over to him with her body at his eye level. HE pours champagne down his pant leg.*)

KEN. I'm sure. I'm sure. I'm really, really sure.

MELISSA. You're spilling on your leg.

KEN. I am? I am! Well. To us.

MELISSA. To us.

(*THEY drink.*)

KEN. Cheers.

MELISSA. Cheers.

(*THEY drink. SHE gulps it.*)

MELISSA. Can I have some more?

KEN. Yes. Yes.

(*KEN pours more champagne. SHE gulps that too. MELISSA stretches out.*)

MELISSA. Are you very limber?

KEN. Pardon me?

MELISSA. You know, limber? I think that's so important in a relationship. Don't you?

KEN. (*Caught up in staring at her.*) What?

MELISSA. Well, I guess you don't really get to stretch out too much selling time-shares, am I right?

KEN. (*Sucks in gut.*) Oh yeah. I work out. Keep trim. But not as much as someone who teaches aerobics.

MELISSA. Not aerobics. "Stretch and Stress Reduction." Big difference.

(*THEY start to kiss.*)

KEN. Big, big difference.

MELISSA. Oh, Ken. I really feel this night is going to be so special. Our lives will never be the same.

KEN. I sure as hell hope not.

(*HE removes his pants. Places them on the chair. MELISSA is still on the bed. As HE starts to cross back, SHE leaps up and straddles him. THEY start to kiss.*)

KEN. Oh, boy. Oh boy, you *are* limber.

(*THEY kiss.*)

MELISSA. Mm-hm.

KEN. You are so incredibly sexy.

MELISSA. You too. You look just like the guy on the jock itch commercial.

KEN. Different guy.

(THEY kiss. As they do, KEN sees a MAN in a wool hat watching them from outside the window out on the ledge. KEN is startled.)

KEN. What the hell is that?
MELISSA. What?
KEN. There's someone out there.
MELISSA. What? Where?
KEN. Out on the ledge. There's a man out there on the ledge.
MELISSA. Oh, that's just Carl.
KEN. Carl? You know him?
MELISSA. Carl is my ex-boyfriend. We broke up. *(Calls.)* Hi, Carl!

(SHE waves. CARL waves back.)

KEN. What's he doing out there?
MELISSA. I don't know.
KEN. *(Waving for Carl to go away.)* Get off there!

(CARL waves back at Ken.)

KEN. *(Waves even bigger.)* Go away!

(CARL waves back even bigger.)

KEN. This is your ex-boyfriend?
MELISSA. Yeah. We broke up three months ago.
KEN. Does he know that?

MELISSA. Of course he knows that. He said he wanted to see other people.

KEN. Well ... he's seeing me and you right now.

MELISSA. Just ignore him. He'll go away.

KEN. "Ignore him?" I can't ignore him. We're twenty-three stories up.

MELISSA. Wave to him.

KEN. Huh?

MELISSA. Just wave to him. It'll keep him happy. (*SHE waves.*)

KEN. I'm calling security.

MELISSA. Oh, don't do that. He's not hurting anybody.

(*CARL waves back.*)

KEN. Well ... I'm closing the drapes. (*HE does.*)

MELISSA. Bye, Carl!

(*CARL waves back.*)

KEN. What's the matter with him?

MELISSA. He just can't let go.

KEN. Well, I hope not. He's twenty-three floors up. How did he know where you are?

MELISSA. He followed us from the bar.

KEN. He was in the bar the whole time we were in there?

MELISSA. Yes. He sat right next to us. He kept peeking over the top of the booth.

KEN. I never saw him.

MELISSA. He's very shy.

KEN. Is he dangerous?

(MELISSA laughs.)

KEN. Is that funny?
MELISSA. It is if you know Carl.
KEN. I can't believe we coincidentally picked a bar that your ex-boyfriend just happened to be in.
MELISSA. Oh, he knew I'd be there. I told him where I was going tonight.
KEN. You did? Why?
MELISSA. So he wouldn't worry. He stays up late and worries if I don't let him know where I am or if I stay out real late.
KEN. How would he know what time you go home? Does he spy on you across the street or something?
MELISSA. No. Nothing like that.
KEN. Good.
MELISSA. We sort of still live together.
KEN. You said he was your ex-boyfriend.
MELISSA. He is. We broke up.
KEN. You broke up but you still live together.
MELISSA. It was easier than breaking up our salt and pepper shaker collection. So ... anyway ... where were we? *(SHE goes to kiss him.)*
KEN. Wait a minute. I can't do this with him looking over my shoulder.
MELISSA. You closed the drapes.
KEN. Just a minute. *(HE opens the drapes and looks out.)* Omigod. He's gone.
MELISSA. Told you.
KEN. You don't suppose he fell?

MELISSA. I doubt it. He has webbed feet. He sticks to practically any surface. And besides, he's very limber.

KEN. Melissa, I don't know if this is such a good idea...

MELISSA. Oh, come on. Don't you want to...?

(KEN checks over his shoulder, then looks her sexy body up and down.)

MELISSA. Cause I really, really want to, Ken ...

KEN. Well ... okay ...

(THEY start to kiss. KEN peeks at the window for Carl. Nothing. THEY move to the bed.
SFX: TELEPHONE)

KEN. Hello? Hello? (*KEN hangs up.*)
KEN. Hang up.
MELISSA. That was Carl.
KEN. Carl? How do you know?
MELISSA. He hates to talk on the phone.
KEN. What does he want?
MELISSA. What do any of us really want? He just wants to be loved.
KEN. Well ... tell him to get his own girl.
MELISSA. I already did. There's just no talking to Carl.
KEN. I guess not.
MELISSA. I hope you didn't hurt his feelings.

KEN. *His* feelings? What about my feelings? Look, Melissa, when we met tonight I didn't know this was a package deal. Love me love my Carl ....

(KNOCK at the door.)

MELISSA. That's him.
KEN. Oh, for God's sake. *(Calls.)* Carl? Carl? *(To Melissa.)*There's no answer.
MELISSA. That's him all right. He hates to talk to closed doors.
KEN. I'm calling security.

(MELISSA opens the door and CARL enters.)

MELISSA. Hi, Carl. Come on in.
KEN. Hey!
MELISSA. Something wrong?
KEN. Yes ... I don't ...
MELISSA. Carl, this is Ken. Ken, Carl.

(CARL waves.)

KEN. Look, pal.

(CARL goes to the TV and turns it on. HE sits down and watches TV.)

KEN. What's he doing ... Where is he ... Is there ... *(To Carl.)* Are your parents brother and sister?

(CARL nods "no.")

KEN. What's the matter with him? (*To Carl.*) Say something. Will you say something? What's the matter with him?

MELISSA. Just wave to him. Say "Hello Carl."

KEN. I am not going to wave and say hello Carl.

(*CARL looks upset.*)

MELISSA. You're hurting his feelings.

KEN. (*Waving his hand half-heartedly.*) "Hello Carl."

(*CARL waves hello.*)

MELISSA. See? He likes you.

KEN. I'm so glad.

(*CARL sits on the edge of the bed.*)

KEN. Where's he going?

MELISSA. Just ignore him.

KEN. Ignore him?

MELISSA. Carl, don't you bother us. We broke up, remember?

(*CARL nods okay.*)

KEN. What is wrong with him?

MELISSA. He just loved me too much. Too long. Too hard. Too deep.

(CARL nods.)

MELISSA. But now I love you.
KEN. Huh? You just met me.
MELISSA. Let's kiss.
KEN. Wait. No. What about Carl?
MELISSA. I don't want to kiss Carl.
KEN. That's not what I meant.
MELISSA. You want to kiss Carl?
KEN. No. I can't kiss you with Carl sitting there watching us. Don't you have any compassion for this guy at all? He's mad about you. Aren't you, Carl?

(CARL nods.)

KEN. He follows you around like a dog. He clings to the sides of buildings to see you. And what do you do? You wave to him and ignore him. Look at him. Will you look at him? You've left him a limp, broken former shadow of himself. Ravaged by jealousy and unrequited love. Don't you have a heart? Don't you have any humanity? Can't you see what this man has been through? *(To Carl.)* It's been rough, Carl. Hasn't it?

(CARL nods.)

KEN. I bet it has, Carl. I understand.
MELISSA. Hey! Come on. That's enough socializing with Carl. *(MELISSA climbs on Ken's lap.)* Pay some attention to me.
KEN. Melissa. Please. Not in front of Carl.

MELISSA. Hey. This is my date, Carl. I hate when this happens.

KEN. This has happened before?

(CARL nods.)

MELISSA. Once or twice.

(CARL motions seven times.)

KEN. Seven times? *(To Melissa.)* How can you do this? I am shocked, and yes, a little disappointed in you.

MELISSA. This doesn't sound like you, Ken.

KEN. What do you mean this doesn't sound like me? You just met me two hours ago.

MELISSA. You're starting to sound just like Carl.

KEN. How can I sound like Carl? Carl doesn't make any noise.

(CARL agrees he's got a point.)

MELISSA. You men are all alike. Why do I even waste my time.

KEN. What?

MELISSA. Every time, I think to myself "tonight will be different." But you all side with Carl. Every single time! I'm sorry, Ken. But this is goodbye.

KEN. What?

MELISSA. I'm sorry if this hurts you. But I just don't see how this can ever work out between us.

KEN. I ...

MELISSA. You're just so demanding. And selfish. And you never think of me. All you ever think of are you and Carl. I can't live with a man like that.

KEN. But ...

MELISSA. Shucks. And I really thought we could have had something really, really neat-o. Oh, well. Goodbye, Ken. (*SHE bolts for the door.*) You know where to find me, Carl.

(CARL nods and waves. MELISSA exits. KEN is dazed.)

KEN. Goodbye, Melissa. (*KEN waves.*)

KEN. I feel so used.

(CARL nods. HE motions for Ken to sit. KEN sits. From his back pocket, CARL offers Ken a wool hat. KEN puts it on, THEY watch TV together.)

BLACKOUT

SCENE 2
"The Superstar"

Curtain opens on a darkened hotel suite. TWO FIGURES are seen under the sheets. We hear a MAN'S VOICE.

JACK. I'm sorry. This has never happened to me before.

ANNIE. It's okay. (*Pause.*) Is it me? (*Pause.*) Yes. Yes, I guess it must be, huh? I'm not very experienced with men. (*ANNIE turns on a lamp.*) I'm sorry, Mr. Broderick. God, this must be so embarrassing for you. I've never really seen this happen to a guy before. I've heard stories about it. Usually it involves pathetically drunk guys or men with war wounds or guys who take sex change hormone shots.

But you. You're "Jack Broderick." Who would have guessed you could ever be impotent? Not me. That's for sure. "Rough Guy Jack" movies are my passion. I've seen them all, you know. *Rough Guy Jack, Navy Seal; Rough Guy Jack, Black Belt Crime Cruncher.* But *Rough Guy Jack, Green Beret Commando* is my all-time favorite. God. When I woke up this morning, who would have thought I'd end up in "Rough Guy Jack's" bed? Not me. That's for sure.

And I bet when you got up this morning you never would have guessed you'd end up in bed with Annie Quinn, your number one fan, either. Huh?

I really am your number one fan, you know. And I don't mean that in a stupid *Misery* sort of way. I'm not gonna chop your legs off and make you write novels in my cabin.

But you probably already know that. I bet you recognize my name from all the letters I write you. "Annie Quinn?" I bet that rings a bell. "Annie." You called me "Gladys" before, and I didn't think it was polite to correct you, but it's "Annie."

Hey, you know? I just thought of something. Maybe it's medication! If you're taking medication, impotence could be a side effect. I read that in *Reader's Digest*. "Tagamet" makes you sterile, so anything is possible.

And wine, that's another possibility. Wine dulls the senses, you know. If you drank wine at dinner ... Oh, but you didn't drink any wine at dinner. And I would know because I was your waitress, remember? You drank Evian with a twist of lemon. And then you had crab cakes with extra lemon, remember? Hey! Maybe there's something in lemons.

Wouldn't that be scary? If lemons cause impotency. *The Enquirer* would put you right on the cover: "Impotent Jack Broderick—The Citrus Fruit Connection." It would be, like, a big picture of you in bed with a great big lemon ...

I'm a pretty good waitress. I mean, I guess I have to be. When you didn't leave me a tip but left your actual phone number and hotel room on the receipt ... I knew you must have thought I was pretty good. You don't do this with just any old waitress, do you? Well, you probably do. Just not ones named "Tommy."

(Laughs.)

Didn't know I was funny, did you?

I don't mind. One night with "Jack Broderick" is a dream come true for any girl. Especially this girl. All my girlfriends know how crazy I am about you, too. We have "Jack Broderick Birthday Parties" every April 17, "Mr. Aries." Me and Felicia and Rhonda and Judy. And they don't even like your movies. But we have a good time. "Mindless sexist trash." That's what they think of your films. But I don't care. I know art when I see it. They only like Jerry Lewis in France too, you know.

But it's funny. You sure make love different in the movies, don't you? I mean, not "ha ha" funny. But funny nonetheless. I mean, who would have guessed.

God, can you imagine Kevin Costner or Tom Cruise or Mel Gibson actually being impotent in one of their movies? Like right in the middle of a passionate love scene, hearing one of them say "I'm sorry, this has never happened to me before?"

I think people might laugh. I could see it in a Pee Wee Herman movie, though. Now, that would be a riot. I should write to him and suggest he do that. I wouldn't even charge him. He could just use my idea. That's kind of how I am.

You know what's odd? It never happens in your "Rough Guy Jack" films either, you realize that? And you sleep with everybody. It's true. In the movies, men are never impotent—unless they fall in radioactive waste or something. You never fell in any radioactive waste, did you?

No, of course not. I would have read about it. Hey, what will happen if you do a love scene in your next movie and this happens again? Would you have to use, like, a stunt man? No, I guess not. They only film you from the back. Pretty lucky, huh?

My girlfriend Felicia was with this one guy and he couldn't ... you know ... what happened to you happened to him too, but she found out it was because the guy was gay.

And he had only picked her up because he thought she was a man. She has a little facial hair, you know? It wasn't the first time somebody thought that of her.

So, I'd say the guy had a pretty good excuse for not getting turned on, wouldn't you? Can you imagine going to bed with somebody and finding out they thought you were a man?

(Gasps.)

God. I hope you didn't think I was a man. (*Pause.*) I didn't think you were a woman, in case you were wondering.

(Laughs.)

There I go again. Miss Class Clown.
You know, actually this isn't the first time this has happened to me. But the other time didn't really count because this guy was real drunk, so I don't know if he could do it or not. He just cried and cried and cried. And then he threw up on me.

(Peers over at him.)

You're not going to cry or throw up, are you? I probably would. I'd cry. I'd cry a lot.
Maybe we should call a doctor. What do you think? 'Cause, you know, I've been looking forward to this night all my life and it just, well, it seems like such a gyp.
No. You're right. We shouldn't call anyone. We don't want your name in the papers. It could hurt your image.
This is fine. Really. It is. It's a nice night. The room is so lovely. You gave me those little honey roasted nuts and that glass of water and that mint. That was a nice touch.

This is better than my wildest dreams. It is exciting just to be here with you.

(JACK snores.)

No one's ever going to believe this, you know. I can't wait to write it in my diary and tell everybody. I'll just leave my diary open on my dresser and let my mother find it when she makes my bed. Yes, I know. I still live at home. Don't you rib me like all my girlfriends do. But what can I do? It would take me years to take down the wall collage I made of your magazine fan photos anyway.

(Sighs.)

I wonder how many other fans have written about you in their diaries. Millions of lucky women like me who get to spend one fleeting night with the great Jack Broderick.

But, hey, you know? The more I think about tonight and how you say this has never happened to you before ... well, it makes me kind of special, you know? I'm your first sexual failure. It's an honor. A true honor. It makes me unique. You can sleep with any girl you want. But not with me. I'm special. I'm a special girl.

And just think. Every time this happens to you in the future you'll think of me. "Annie Quinn."

I will treasure this memory, Mr. Broderick.

(JACK snores.)

Oh, Jack. You've made me your one special girl. This is the happiest night of my life! Good night, my sweet prince! This is the best sex I've ever had!

(JACK snores. ANNIE turns off the LIGHT and goes to sleep.)

BLACKOUT

SCENE 3
"The Blue Movie"

A sexy WOMAN, dressed in a sexy robe, opens her hotel door and lets in a young BELLHOP. The picture on the TV flips in the background.

ERIKKA. Thanks for coming. There seems to be something wrong with the television set.
BELLBOY. You don't want it to flip up and down like that?
ERIKKA. No.
BELLBOY. Oh. Well, then. I guess you're right. Let's just take a look, shall we?
ERIKKA. I hope it's not broken.
BELLBOY. (*Goes to the TV.*) Ah, I see. Mm-hm.
ERIKKA. Is it serious?
BELLBOY. You've got the set on the wrong channel.
ERIKKA. I do?

BELLBOY. Yes. See? See how it's flipping? If you keep the TV on channel three, then the cable box works just fine. No flipping.

ERIKKA. Oh, yes. God, you're smart.

BELLBOY. A lot of people get confused. All fixed.

ERIKKA. My God, what strong hands you have.

BELLBOY. How's that?

ERIKKA. You're so strong to fix an entire television with your bare hands.

BELLBOY. I just pressed the button. It's nothing.

ERIKKA. And you knew exactly what button to press.

BELLBOY. All part of the job. They train us very well here.

ERIKKA. Yes, they do. Thank you so much. Now, stay right here. I want to give you a little something.

BELLBOY. Oh, sure. Thank you, Ma'am.

(SHE exits to the bathroom. The BELLBOY looks around. HE sees fifty cents on the bureau. HE steals it and pockets it. Next HE sees several sexy negligees on the bed. HE holds them up one by one. ERIKKA enters. HE is caught with a negligee. HE stuffs it down his pants.)

ERIKKA. Miss me?

BELLBOY. Huh? Oh, yeah.

ERIKKA. I can't seem to find my purse ...

BELLBOY. Oh, well. No matter. It's always a pleasure to help a beautiful lady.

ERIKKA. Really?

BELLBOY. In fact, if there is anything else I can do for you before I leave, please let me know.

ERIKKA. I'd love a drink.
BELLBOY. A drink?
ERIKKA. I don't know how to work the bar.
BELLBOY. Oh. It's really simple. You just take what you want out of the bar, and when the maid cleans up she'll restock it and charge you for what's missing. What would you like?
ERIKKA. Vodka. (*Husky voiced.*) And ice.
BELLBOY. Ah. Allow me. Here you go. One vodka and ice. (*HE mixes her a drink.*)
ERIKKA. You stir with such force.
BELLBOY. I what?
ERIKKA. Would you like something to drink?
BELLBOY. I can't. Thank you. I'm working. I'd lose my job.
ERIKKA. Who would know?
BELLBOY. Well, I guess one drink wouldn't hurt. Especially if I have a mint afterwards.

(*HE laughs. SHE laughs. HE puts ice in a glass for himself.*)

ERIKKA. Oh, my. This is going right to my head.
BELLBOY. Well, that is understandable. It is a little warm in here.
ERIKKA. Yes, it is.

(*SHE removes her robe. SHE wears a corset. The BELLBOY misses his glass with ice.*)

BELLBOY. I could open a window.
ERIKKA. They don't open.

BELLBOY. (*Absent-mindedly pounding on the window*.) What?

ERIKKA. They don't open. You're starting to perspire.

BELLBOY. I am? (*HE pounds on the window some more*.)

ERIKKA. Are all the bellhops as adorable as you?

BELLBOY. No, I think I'm the only one. (*HE pounds some more*.)

ERIKKA. I don't seem to be able to find my change purse. Is there any other way I can thank you?

BELLBOY. Mm. Gee. I can't think of any way.

ERIKKA. Let me see ...

BELLBOY. Oh, there's no need to "see." This drink is quite a thank you, let me tell you. (*HE chews the ice like an idiot*.)

ERIKKA. I know! It isn't much, but maybe this will suffice.

(*SHE grabs him and kisses him passionately. His DRINK shakes and the ICE flies out all over the room*.)

ERIKKA. (*Spitting out an ice cube*.) I hope that was okay.

BELLBOY. Huh?

ERIKKA. I said I hope that was okay.

BELLBOY. What?

ERIKKA. This. (*SHE does it again. Then:*)

BELLBOY. Oh. Yeah.

ERIKKA. I'm so glad. Then I suppose this would be okay, too.

(SHE kisses him harder. SHE breaks the kiss, pulls down his pants and falls back on the bed. HE is dazed.)

ERIKKA. Make me glad I'm a woman!
BELLBOY. What?
ERIKKA. I said, make me glad I'm a woman.

(SHE lays back down. The BELLBOY is speechless.)

BELLBOY. Well ... you don't have to wear a cup when you play softball.
ERIKKA. No. Take me. Have your way with me. Leave no stone unturned.
BELLBOY. You ... you have stones?
ERIKKA. Take me.
BELLBOY. Well ... okay then ... *(HE takes a step towards her. HE trips on the pants and falls.)*

(CUBBY SPICONI enters from the other room. HE carries a video camera and a tripod.)

CUBBY. That was great!
BELLBOY. *(Clutches at his pants.)* What?
ERIKKA. Cubby!
BELLBOY. Who are you?
CUBBY. Cubby Spiconi.
ERIKKA. My husband.
BELLBOY. Your husband? Where did he come from?
CUBBY. Des Moines.
BELLBOY. I ... uh ... I can explain.
ERIKKA. *(To Cubby.)* He'll be great.

CUBBY. I think so, too. Cubby Spiconi. Nice to meet you. I see you've met my wife.

BELLBOY. What? Hey, look, mister. I didn't mean ...

CUBBY. No need to get dressed. Call me Cubby.

BELLBOY. What do you mean?

CUBBY. Instead of Mr. Spiconi. Call me Cubby.

BELLBOY. What are you talking about?

ERIKKA. You're scaring him, Cubby.

BELLBOY. "Cubby?" Omigod. You're not the kid from the Mickey Mouse Club, are you?

CUBBY. Funny guy. Hold this. I gotta adjust the lighting.

*(CUBBY hands the bellboy the video camera. HE adjusts a
    desk lamp.)*

BELLBOY. What is this?

CUBBY. Video camera. And may I say, you look great on film. Anybody ever tell you that?

BELLBOY. What?

ERIKKA. And he's not even wearing any makeup.

CUBBY. (*Taking back the camera.*) You're right. Thanks. I got some in the bathroom you can use. I'm the makeup man, too.

BELLBOY. You're a what?

CUBBY. Remember to keep your hair out of your eyes, Erikka.

ERIKKA. Sorry.

BELLBOY. What's going on here?

CUBBY. Pretty sexy, isn't she?

BELLBOY. Who?

CUBBY. "Who?" How many beautiful women do you see in the room?

BELLBOY. (*Looking around.*) Well ...

CUBBY. Her! Sexy as hell.

BELLBOY. Yes. No. I didn't notice.

CUBBY. You noticed. You noticed plenty. You want me to play the tape back for you?

BELLBOY. Tape?

CUBBY. The videotape.

BELLBOY. You filmed me? Us?

CUBBY. Your left side's the best angle.

ERIKKA. Good. That's better for me. He's great, Cubby. Very sexy and he even looks like a Viking.

CUBBY. I know. It's perfect. You got black socks on? Great.

BELLBOY. I look like a what?

CUBBY. A Viking. We need a Viking. A Viking with black socks.

BELLBOY. I'm not a Viking. I'm a bellboy.

CUBBY. We'll stick a hat on you. Who's gonna know?

ERIKKA. Have you ever done any acting?

BELLBOY. Acting?

CUBBY. We're making a little film here, see? I'm the producer, the director, the cameraman, the script writer. Erikka's the star.

BELLBOY. She's the star...?

CUBBY. You recognize her?

BELLBOY. Sorry. I ...

ERIKKA. That's okay.

BELLBOY. I ... I don't get out much. You do look familiar. But I ...

CUBBY. Erikka's a big star, believe you me. She's been in two other films we made together. *The Butt-inski* and my personal favorite *I Said I Wanted a Butt Light.*

BELLBOY. Oh, yeah. I heard of that one. In fact, I'm gonna go catch it. I'm gonna go catch it right now. (*HE starts to leave.*)

ERIKKA. Where are you going?

BELLBOY. I'm going to go catch it.

CUBBY. No, you're not.

BELLBOY. Look, I don't know what you two are into here, but I'm out of here.

ERIKKA. Oh. Don't go. Please.

CUBBY. Come on, Man. The adult video scene is happening.

BELLBOY. Look ... you may be happening, but I'm working. Now, I'd love to stay here and do unnatural things with mules on film for you, but ... I got a job.

CUBBY. Yeah. That's right. Your job. Tsk. Tsk. Tsk. I wouldn't want you to lose it.

BELLBOY. Why would I lose my job?

CUBBY. (*Tapping videocamera.*) Don't do the film, lose your job. Do the film, keep your job.

BELLBOY. I'm not acting in any porno movie.

ERIKKA. Adult video.

BELLBOY. I'm not acting in any adult video, either.

CUBBY. You want me to show this footage to your hotel manager? They got a policy against fraternization with the guests. And drinking while on duty. And if I'm not mistaken you stole fifty cents off my bureau.

BELLBOY. You filmed me ... drinking and ... stealing...?

CUBBY. You're reprehensible.

BELLBOY. I don't want to do this.

CUBBY. Don't worry about a thing. We'll keep it all our little secret. We don't even have to use your real name. And you'll have a hat on.

ERIKKA. That's how we got our last two leading men.

BELLBOY. With hats?

CUBBY. We love this hotel. It's so easy to recruit actors here. *Butt-inski* starred one of your room service guys. I think he was an illegal alien. He said yes right away. Manuel something. We changed his name to Johnny Studdman for the film. He's a big star now.

ERIKKA. We had to teach him the dialogue phonetically. But his moaning is universal.

CUBBY. This film is a period piece.

BELLBOY. A what?

CUBBY. A Scandinavian sex fantasy called *The Savage Vikings Fight Over Freya*. Erikka is the Nordic Goddess Freya. You play Odr. One of the Savage Vikings.

BELLBOY. "Odor?"

CUBBY. O-D-R. We stick a block of Swiss Cheese on the headboard and this room becomes the Palace Sessrumnir. And since I couldn't find any dwarfs for the festival scene, I'll be playing that myself on my knees in a beard.

ERIKKA. He always does cameos like Alfred Hitchcock used to do.

CUBBY. It's a kick. And the fans look for it.

BELLBOY. What exactly do I have to do?

ERIKKA. Make mad passionate Viking love while my husband videotapes you.

BELLBOY. I don't feel so good.

CUBBY. It's just nerves. Remember your first time, Erikka?

ERIKKA. No. Not really.

CUBBY. Well, I do. You were nervous, believe you me. She sweat like a pig. You'll see. A couple of hours of this and you'll be just fine.

BELLBOY. Couple of hours?

CUBBY. You're good for a couple of takes, aren't you?

BELLBOY. I don't think so.

ERIKKA. You'll be fine.

CUBBY. (*Filming himself talking into camera.*) "Savage Vikings. Scene One. Take One." Okay, places everybody.

BELLBOY. Wait a minute. Wait a minute. We can't do this. You said "Savage Vikings?" How can there be Savage Vikings when I'm the only Viking?

CUBBY. (*Calls.*) Lyle, are you ready yet?

(*LYLE enters from the bathroom. A thirty-five-year-old loser. HE is dressed in a fur toga and a viking hat. HE carries an open magazine.*)

LYLE. I'm doing the best I can. The news stand was out of *Playboy* Magazines. I've had to make do with the Room Service menu.

BELLBOY. The what?

CUBBY. Lyle meet Odr. Odr, Lyle.

LYLE. Hi.

BELLBOY. What part of the hotel do you work in?

LYLE. I don't work in the hotel.

CUBBY. Lyle's my brother-in-law.

ERIKKA. He played the Coal Miner in *Butt Light*. And the Nosy Neighbor in *Butt-inski*.

BELLBOY. You're in all these movies?

LYLE. It's more fun than bowling.

BELLBOY. I'm nauseous.

CUBBY. It's just your adrenalin.

BELLBOY. Well ... my adrenalin wants to throw up.

CUBBY. What do you have to be nervous about? If anybody should be nervous, it's Lyle.

LYLE. That's right. If people in my parish find out about this I could get thrown out of the church.

CUBBY. Okay, let's get started here.

BELLBOY. I feel sick to my stomach.

ERIKKA. It'll help with your moaning. (*ERIKKA pulls out a viking helmet and a tunic.*)

BELLBOY. Omigod.

ERIKKA. Here's your hat, and fur tunic.

BELLBOY. What if someone walks in ...

(*ERIKKA dresses the Bellboy in the fur tunic.*)

CUBBY. Keep your socks and shoes on.

BELLBOY. I can't ... I couldn't ... I'm not the right guy for this. I'm ... I'm ... terrible with accents. Especially Scandinavian accents ... I ...

ERIKKA. Yust say "Ya" a lot. "Ya, Ya, Ya! I am Freya the Nordic goddess, ya!"

CUBBY. God. She's like Meryl Streep. That accent's so authentic I got a chill.

LYLE. Come on. Let's get started. I have to get back to the church. It's Vespers Service tonight.

BELLBOY. I'm getting dizzy.

*(CUBBY gets the script out. ERIKKA hands the Bellboy a
    red beard and an ax.)*

CUBBY. Then lean against the wall. You're not in the
first scene.

(The BELLBOY leans.)

CUBBY. Okay. First set-up. The lovely Freya is found
weeping in the woods.
BELLBOY. What woods?
ERIKKA. He's right. We don't have any woods.
CUBBY. Oh, yeah. Okay. Stand by the window. I can
get a piece of Central Park over your shoulder.

(ERIKKA poses. LYLE readies for his entrance.)

ERIKKA. How's this?
CUBBY. That's hot, baby. Okay, Lyle. You come
upon her and want to ravage her. Ready, everybody?
ERIKKA. Yeah.
LYLE. Yeah.
CUBBY. And ... action!
ERIKKA. "Ya, ya. I am so sad. To be outzen in der
woodzen."

*(SHE weeps into her hands, shaking her breasts. LYLE
    comes upon her. As he speaks HE slaps at his feet like
    a Swiss Alps yodeler.)*

LYLE. "Ya. Ya. You lookin a little tensen. Shall I rubben your shoulders, ya?"
ERIKKA. "Ya. Ya "

(THEY start to kiss.)

CUBBY. Cut!! There's a window washer. *(Yells off.)* What are you looking at, you pervert? Close the drapes, Lyle.

(LYLE does.)

CUBBY. We'll come back to this scene later. So much for editing in the camera. Next set-up. Scene Two. The Palace Sessrumnir.
ERIKKA. You're on, Odr.
BELLBOY. Damn that window washer. Damn him to hell.
CUBBY. Set dressing! Lyle, put the cheese by the headboard. Okay. Here's the scenario. The beautiful Freya is in bed with the Nordic god Frey.
LYLE. I'm Frey.
BELLBOY. Good.

(LYLE gets into the bed.)

CUBBY. Okay. Odr ... You barge in. You see them together. Frey's having his wanton way with Freya.
BELLBOY. What does that mean, "wanton way?"
LYLE. I get to do whatevèr I'm wantin'.

(CUBBY and LYLE laugh.)

CUBBY. Odr! You see them. You get insanely jealous. Yet, quietly aroused. Then ... after watching them make love like sex-starved snow rabbits, you pull Frey off of Freya. You caress her womanliness, then throw Frey to the ground like a used Scandinavian Kleenex. And then, holding your mighty ax in your hand, the two of you make love. Savage love. Savage dirty love. Lots of dirty Nordic curse words and grunting. Nordic grunting. You can't have enough grunting for me.
LYLE. He's not kidding.
CUBBY. Let me hear you grunt.
BELLBOY. I don't ... I can't ... grunt.
LYLE. It's easy. (*HE demonstrates.*)
CUBBY. He's good, isn't he?
BELLBOY. Yeah. Good grunt.
LYLE. Thanks. (*Grunts again.*)
CUBBY. Try it, Odr.
BELLBOY. No. I'll feel silly. I can't do that.
CUBBY. Yes, you can.
BELLBOY. No, I really ... I ...
CUBBY. You could as least try it.
ERIKKA. Try it, Odr.
LYLE. Try it, Odr.
BELLBOY. Well, okay ...

(*The BELLBOY tries and wheezes.*)

CUBBY. Well ...
LYLE. That's not a grunt. That's a wheeze.
ERIKKA. I think it sounded promising.

CUBBY. It will work. Vikings are known for their wheezing as well as their grunting.

LYLE. I didn't know that.

BELLBOY. I heard that.

CUBBY. Okay. Adult video history is ready to be made. Places. Here we go.

(LYLE and ERIKKA take their places on the bed. The BELLBOY stands off to the side.)

CUBBY. And ... action!

ERIKKA. *(To Lyle.)* "Ya, ya. Make love to me like the sex-starved snow rabbit that you are."

LYLE. "Ya, ya. You lookin a little tensen. Shall I rubben your back, ya?"

ERIKKA. "Ya, ya!"

(THEY make out. CUBBY cues the Bellboy to enter.)

CUBBY. Psst. Psst. Go. Go! Move. Move!

(LYLE moves around wildly.)

CUBBY. Not you, Lyle. Go, Odr. Enter!

BELLBOY. *(Pulls beard off.)* Wait a minute. I can't do it. I just can't.

CUBBY. Cut!! What's the matter with you? Get in there and start ravaging.

BELLBOY. I can't.

LYLE. You need the room service menu?

BELLBOY. No.

ERIKKA. What's the problem, honey?

BELLBOY. I just can't do this.

CUBBY. What part can't you do? You pull Frey off of Freya. You throw him to the ground, you hold your ax in the air and the two of you make savage love. What's the problem?

BELLBOY. It's that last part. I can't have sex with your wife while you film me. It's sick. I can't ...

CUBBY. Not with my wife! You and Lyle!

(The BELLBOY reacts.)

CUBBY. Boy, is he thick. I'll be right back. I gotta get more film. *(CUBBY exits to the bathroom.)*

BELLBOY. "Me and Lyle?" What did he mean, me and Lyle?

ERIKKA. You ravage Lyle.

BELLBOY. I ravage who?

LYLE. You ravage me.

BELLBOY. Wait a second. Wait a Nordic second here. Me and Lyle??

ERIKKA. Why, yes. What did you think he meant?

BELLBOY. I am not doing anything with Lyle!

LYLE. Is it my feet?

BELLBOY. No!

LYLE. Was it something I said?

BELLBOY. *(To Erikka.)* I thought I had to sleep with you!

ERIKKA. Oh, no. My husband would never allow that.

BELLBOY. He what?

LYLE. Are you kidding? Nobody sleeps with Erikka in these films.

ERIKKA. Of course not.

BELLBOY. Never?

ERIKKA. No. Never.

BELLBOY. Let me get this straight. You make porno films without ever having sex in them?

ERIKKA. Of course not, silly. Everybody else has sex in them. Just not me.

BELLBOY. Well ... that doesn't seem very fair.

ERIKKA. That's too bad.

BELLBOY. I never heard of this!

ERIKKA. You sound disappointed.

BELLBOY. No! I'm not ... but ...

ERIKKA. I thought you didn't want to do anything with me anyway.

BELLBOY. I don't. But. Gee. What kind of a porno star are you? You don't even have sex?

ERIKKA. God. You make me feel so cheap.

(CUBBY enters with another tape. HE overhears them talking.)

BELLBOY. Don't you even want to make these movies?

ERIKKA. Not really.

BELLBOY. "Not really?" Then why do you do these terrible things?

ERIKKA. For Cubby. He wants me to do them.

CUBBY. The hell I do. You think I like my wife doing blue movies with strange weirdo bellboys and Lyle?

ERIKKA. You don't?

CUBBY. It turns my stomach.

ERIKKA. Then why do we make these awful degrading films?

CUBBY. I thought you liked them.

ERIKKA. I don't like them.

CUBBY. You said it was your ultimate fantasy "having sex on film."

ERIKKA. Well, yes, Cubby. But I meant you and me. You always take things to extremes.

CUBBY. God, all these years I was only doing this for you.

ERIKKA. And I was only doing it for you.

(ERIKKA and CUBBY kiss. The BELLBOY walks away from them. HE bumps into Lyle.)

LYLE. I was doing it because I liked doing it.

CUBBY. (*Breaking kiss.*) Okay, everybody. I have an announcement to make. Erikka's not going to be in the film anymore.

ERIKKA. Do you mean it?

CUBBY. You know I do.

(THEY kiss.)

BELLBOY. I think you've come to the right decision. You don't want to degrade yourself like that.

ERIKKA. You're right.

CUBBY. He's right.

ERIKKA. Oh. But, Cubby. You already paid for the room and had these expensive costumes made.

CUBBY. It's okay. I'll just rewrite. Now we'll call it *The Two Golden Viking Boys.* Starring Odr and Lyle!

ERIKKA. Yes!

LYLE. Second billing? Wow!

BELLBOY. What? Wait.

CUBBY. I can see it all now. We open in the woods with Odr openly weeping because he's realized his life as a ladies man was nothing but a sham.

BELLBOY. Huh?

CUBBY. He knows he isn't attracted to the goddess Freya in that special way anymore, ever since he took that trip to the Baths.

BELLBOY. What? Wait a second ...

CUBBY. Before he can wipe away his last tear, the manly wood nymph Frey skips along and asks:

LYLE. (*To Bellboy.*) "Ya. Ya. You lookin a little tensen. Shall I rubben your shoulders, ya ya?"

BELLBOY. Ya nothing! That's it. That is it! I am out of here!

ERIKKA. Odr, wait!

BELLBOY. No way.

LYLE. Is it my feet?

BELLBOY. No!

CUBBY. What about your job?

BELLBOY. I don't give a red hot Scandinavian damn! You can keep your tunic and your ax and your lousy stinkin' itchin' beard and especially your horn helmet ... I am history! (*The BELLBOY bolts for the door.*)

LYLE. Wait. Odr? Wait! Before you go ...

BELLBOY. Yeah?

LYLE. Want to go bowling sometime?

BELLBOY. No!

(*The BELLBOY runs out the door. There is a pause. CUBBY, ERIKKA and LYLE suddenly can't hold it in any longer and break up laughing.*)

CUBBY. That was a good one!

LYLE. (*Clocking the Bellboy's exit.*) He lasted ten minutes and thirty-five seconds! (*Consulting pad on desk.*) Erikka wins.

ERIKKA. Pay up.

(CUBBY and LYLE pay her five bucks a piece.)

ERIKKA. (*Laughing.*) Did you see his face? (*Imitating the Bellboy in mock shock.*) "Me and Lyle?"

LYLE. (*Laughing.*) "You make porno movies and never have sex?"

CUBBY. "Want me to be rubbin' your shoulders, ya ya?"

(THEY laugh hard. Their laughing dies down.)

ERIKKA. Again?

LYLE. Yeah! This time I want to be the director.

CUBBY. Okay. And we'll pretend Erikka's married to you.

ERIKKA. (*Keeping score on the pad.*) I say the next one lasts fifteen minutes, thirty seconds.

LYLE. Ten minutes, twenty seconds.

CUBBY. Two minutes flat. I'm answering the door!

(ERIKKA dials the phone.)

LYLE. Let's make the next one a Gaelic fairy porno movie.

CUBBY. Great. Do we have any stupid Celtic costumes for the next schmuck?

(CUBBY and LYLE get the room ready.)

ERIKKA. Hello? Front desk? This is Mrs. Spiconi in 2312. There seems to be something wrong with my TV. Could you send someone up to take a look at it? Thank you.

CURTAIN

ACT II

SCENE 1
"The Wedding"

A tuxedoed MAN and a MAID OF HONOR frolic on the bed. THEY are dressed but quite disheveled.

WALTER. Claudia ... please. Please. We have to get downstairs.

CLAUDIA. Not yet.

WALTER. Claudia, please. The wedding was supposed to start fifteen minutes ago.

CLAUDIA. Nobody's wedding ever starts on time.

WALTER. But ... we have guests ... people are waiting.

CLAUDIA. Let 'em wait.

WALTER. They'll be wondering.

CLAUDIA. Let them wonder.

WALTER. But ... but our parents are down there and...!

CLAUDIA. Walter, my mother's waited twenty-six years for this wedding. She can wait fifteen more minutes.

WALTER. You're an animal, Claudia.

CLAUDIA. I don't care, Walter. I'll never see you after today.

WALTER. How can you say that? I'm marrying your sister. I'll see you all the time.

CLAUDIA. Yes, but it can never be the same between us, after you and Wendy say "I do." There's a line I just won't cross.

(KNOCK at the door.)

MRS. KIRSCHENBAUM. (*Off.*) Walter Saltzman? You open this door right this minute.
CLAUDIA. It's my mother!
WALTER. I told you we were late!
CLAUDIA. What do we do?
WALTER. Uh ... Don't panic. Just don't panic. (*Calls.*) I'll be right there, Mrs. Kirschenbaum! (*To Claudia.*) Get dressed and go out through the adjoining room. Quick!

(WALTER quickly buttons his shirt up. CLAUDIA is perplexed.)

CLAUDIA. I can't.
WALTER. What do you mean you can't?
CLAUDIA. We're stuck!
WALTER. What do you mean we're stuck? Stuck how?
CLAUDIA. Stuck-Stuck.
WALTER. You mean, like dogs-stuck?
CLAUDIA. No! Stuck like your zipper is caught in my taffeta-stuck.
WALTER. Are you kidding?
CLAUDIA. Hey, watch it. Don't rip my dress. Wendy will kill me!
WALTER. Okay. Listen to me. Panic.

(KNOCK at the door.)

MRS. KIRSCHENBAUM. Open this door, Mr. Saltzman!

WALTER. I'm dead. I'm dead. I'm a dead man.

CLAUDIA. Oh, and I suppose I'm not a dead man?

WALTER. I know. Get on top of me and say "come in."

CLAUDIA. Now? Now, you want me to get on top of you?

WALTER. Don't be a pig, Claudia. Will you just do it?

(KNOCK at the door.)

MRS. KIRSCHENBAUM. *(Off.)* Open this door, Walter! I have a key and I'm coming in! I know you're in there! It's Mrs. Kirschenbaum!

WALTER. Hurry up.

(WALTER lays down, CLAUDIA sits on the bed. WALTER drapes the bedspread over his torso, leaving his legs dangling off the bed like they're coming out of Claudia's skirt. Walter's pant legs are hiked up, revealing black socks and garters. And hairy legs. MRS. KIRSCHENBAUM enters.)

MRS. KIRSCHENBAUM. Claudia! Where the hell is Walter?

CLAUDIA. He ... left. Through the adjoining room. You must have just passed him in the hall.

MRS. KIRSCHENBAUM. What are you doing up here?

(WALTER'S arm pops out through Claudia's arm hole.)

CLAUDIA. I came up to look for Walter.
MRS. KIRSCHENBAUM. Well, he just left. Get downstairs. People are starting to snicker. Old Mrs. Goldfarb has run out of songs to sing. When I left the room she was starting a Springsteen medley. This wedding is a fiasco!

(WALTER "yakity-yaks" with his hand, through Claudia's arm hole. SHE slaps "Walter's" hand.)

MRS. KIRSCHENBAUM. Don't you make fun of me, young lady! (*Gasps.*) Good God, Claudia, look at your legs. And after all your father and I spent on electrolysis.
CLAUDIA. I know, Mom.
MRS. KIRSCHENBAUM. Did it grow back on your shoulders, too?
CLAUDIA. No, Mom.
MRS. KIRSCHENBAUM. Well, my God, Claudia! We have three doctors, two lawyers and seven accountants downstairs. All single. The least you can do is shave your legs. Who knows when I'll get you another opportunity like this?

(MRS. KIRSCHENBAUM leans over to get a shaving kit off the desk. WALTER thumbs Claudia's nose.)

MRS. KIRSCHENBAUM. Here. Use Walter's shaving kit.

CLAUDIA. But Mom. Hairy legs are the latest rage.

MRS. KIRSCHENBAUM. No. *(Indicates herself.)* Here's your latest rage. *(Handing Claudia electric razor.)* Look, Claudia Rachel Kirschenbaum, you know your sister's throwing you the bouquet! And I'll be damned if I'll let all those single men watch them put a garter on my monkey legged daughter. Here.

WALTER. *(Off.)* No!

MRS. KIRSCHENBAUM. Did you say no to me?

CLAUDIA. No. I said yes.

MRS. KIRSCHENBAUM. It sounded like "no."

CLAUDIA. I have dyslexia.

MRS. KIRSCHENBAUM Start shaving!

(CLAUDIA's mouth is open but WALTER's voice comes out.)

WALTER. *(Off.)* No!

CLAUDIA. There I go again. Well, here goes nothing...

(CLAUDIA shaves Walter's legs. WALTER's screams come from CLAUDIA's accommodatingly open mouth. WALTER keeps kicking his legs. MRS. KIRSCHENBAUM's eyes bug out as SHE watches.)

WALTER. *(Off.)* Oooowwww ... oh-oh-oh-oh-ow, you're killing me ... stop it. Oh-oh-oh ... Mm!!!!

MRS. KIRSCHENBAUM. What did you say?

CLAUDIA. Nothing. I just said ...

(SHE shaves his legs again. HE screams all over again.)

WALTER. *(Off.)* Oooowwww … oh-oh-oh-oh-ow, you're killing me … stop it. Oh-oh-oh … Mm!!!!

MRS. KIRSCHENBAUM. Well, what is that supposed to mean?

(WALTER pulls Claudia's hair.)

CLAUDIA. Ow!

MRS. KIRSCHENBAUM. What is the matter with you?

CLAUDIA. I keep nicking myself. Take that!

(SHE shaves more, WALTER struggles and screams.)

WALTER. *(Off)* Oooowwww … oh-oh-oh-oh-oh-oh-oh … Mm!!!!

(WALTER stuffs his fingers up her nose.)

CLAUDIA. Ow. Ow!

MRS. KIRSCHENBAUM. What the hell is the matter with you? Stop that, Claudia. You did that in the car all the way up here, too. Don't think we all weren't watching.

(WALTER removes his hand. CLAUDIA's returns from behind her back.)

MRS. KIRSCHENBAUM. Come on, let's go. *(SHE grabs Claudia's hand.)*

CLAUDIA. Wait a second. You ... uh ... don't want to go downstairs looking like that. Do you, Mom?
MRS. KIRSCHENBAUM Like what?
CLAUDIA. Your makeup is all smeared.

(WALTER's hand wipes across Mrs. Kirschenbaum's face. Her lipstick smears. SHE looks in the mirror.)

MRS. KIRSCHENBAUM. It is? Omigod. I look like your Aunt Fran when she eats grapes. Where's the bathroom?

(SHE exits into the bathroom. WALTER and CLAUDIA climb off the bed.)

CLAUDIA. *(Calls.)* Take your time, Mom!
WALTER. *(To Claudia.)* You shaved my leg!
CLAUDIA. You picked my nose!
WALTER. You had hair on your back?
CLAUDIA. Quick. Take your pants off. I can go borrow tux pants from a waiter and come back for you.

(WALTER takes his pants off. RABBI HUCHELMAN enters just as Walter is de-pantsed. The RABBI sees Claudia and a pantless Walter holding Walter's pants in the air.)

RABBI. Walter?
WALTER. Rabbi Huchelman?
RABBI. Did I come at a bad time?
WALTER. No. What makes you say that?

RABBI. I'm here for the signing of the Katuba. What's with the "no pants?" Is everything all right?

WALTER. Yes. In fact, we were just coming to get you.

CLAUDIA. We were? I mean, we were. We were.

RABBI. Then it's a good thing I wasn't there.

WALTER. You see, everyone knows there's a prayer for the wine and a prayer for the bread, but we have an old family wedding custom where we pray over the pants.

RABBI. Over the pants?

WALTER. Sort of a "go forth and multiply" sort of thing.

RABBI. I never heard of such a thing.

WALTER. Well, it happens.

RABBI. I'm used to the Orthodox.

WALTER. Who isn't?

RABBI. You want me to ...

WALTER. If you don't mind.

RABBI. Not at all.

(HE goes to take the pants. CLAUDIA backs away, clutching the pants.)

CLAUDIA. It's also part of the custom that the maid of honor holds the pants while you pray.

RABBI. I didn't know that.

(As HE prays, MRS. KIRSCHENBAUM enters and sees the scene.)

RABBI. (*Prays.*) May your seed be plentiful. May your offspring follow in the path of the righteous. And may your pants break just right over the tops of your shoes.

MRS. KIRSCHENBAUM. What the hell do you think you're doing?

RABBI. We're praying over the pants.

MRS. KIRSCHENBAUM. I asked you to stay out of the Manischevitz, Rabbi Huchelman.

RABBI. It's an old wedding custom.

MRS. KIRSCHENBAUM. Let me give you a new wedding custom, Huchelman. It's called get downstairs under your tent and stay away from the rum balls. (*SHE shoves HUCHELMAN out the door. To Claudia and Walter.*) And you two better be ready when I come out of the bathroom! (*SHE exits to the bathroom.*)

(*From the adjoining room we hear:*)

WENDY. (*Off.*) Walter? Are you in there?

(*From the adjoining room, WENDY, the distraught bride, sweeps into the room. WALTER hits the floor. WENDY wears her wedding gown with its large train. In a panic, CLAUDIA grabs Wendy's hands and turns her back to WALTER who crawls around trying to find a place to hide.*)

WENDY. (*Crying.*) Oh, Claudia. I don't know what to do. We have a room full of people and everything is such a mess.

CLAUDIA. Wendy, stay down ... calm down.

WENDY. Calm down? Where is he? No one can find him. What am I going to do? I have to find him. We have guests. Aunt Sylvia drove down from Ithaca.

(WALTER panics and crawls under the tablecloth far stage left. HE bulges out ridiculously too much. CLAUDIA sees this and panics.)

CLAUDIA. Walter's not going to stand you up.

(SHE steers WENDY to Walter and hides WALTER under Wendy's train. As WENDY walks around the room, HE will follow her, unseen by Wendy.)

CLAUDIA. He's probably taking care of last minute things. You know. Rehearsing his vows ... getting dressed ... pacing somewhere. You know how he is. He's got his nose into everything.
WENDY. *(Walks stage right. Her "train" follows.)* You don't suppose he changed his mind, do you?
CLAUDIA. Of course not.
WENDY. I'm going to be a laughing stock. The family laughing stock.

(SHE walks stage left, leaving WALTER behind who is unaware she's moved. Still with his eyes covered.)

WENDY. But hey, why should today be any different. I screwed up my entire life so what else is new? Aunt Sylvia is down there laughing at me as it is. And when she laughs, she shakes all the chairs.

*(CLAUDIA sees Walter at the foot of the bed—his eyes
covered. HE is unaware he is in plain sight. CLAUDIA
steers Wendy back to Walter and drapes Wendy's train
over his head.)*

CLAUDIA. We'll find him. Don't worry. He's probably right under your feet somewhere. He's not standing you up.

WENDY. "Standing me up?" I'm not worried he's standing me up.

CLAUDIA. Then what's wrong?

WENDY. I don't know how to say this, Claudia. But I can't keep it in any longer. We went to all this trouble and now everything is all screwed up.

WENDY. *(Walks left again. The "train" follows.)* Mom is going to kill me.

CLAUDIA. What are you trying to say?

WENDY. There's someone else.

CLAUDIA. What do you mean? Walter's having an affair?

WENDY. Worse. *(SHE removes her bouquet and veil drape to reveal a rolled up pair of men's tuxedo pants attached to her gown.)* I am!

*(WENDY walks right. WALTER again is left behind. And
so is a MAN in a tuxedo. This is GLENN.)*

BLACKOUT

SCENE 2
"The Rendezvous"

It is night. The room is set for romance. An offstage SHOWER is heard. The hotel room door opens. A MAN enters.

CRAIG. It's me. I'm here. Honey? (*HE takes off his tie and jacket as he speaks. HE hears the shower. HE checks his watch. HE starts guzzling champagne.*) Loretta? Honey? What are you doing? I can't stay too late tonight. Can you hear me? It's my wife's birthday and I gotta put in an appearance at her party. Which reminds me. I hope the gift shop is still open .... I'm sorry about this. I know how much you look forward to our Monday nights. I hate to do this to you, honey. I'll make it up to you with some of my lunch hours next week. (*HE sees the note, picks it up and reads it.*) What's this? (*HE reads the note.*) "Put this outfit on, blindfold yourself, and lay on the bed." (*Smiles. HE looks around the room and notices all the little romantic touches. HE swaggers around the room.*) Ooh. The hell with the party I'm going to be a naughty boy tonight! Loretta, you're an animal. (*The SHOWER goes off as HE takes off his shirt and pants. HE picks up a beanie with a helicopter top, a big bow tie and saddle shoes. HE puts them on. HE lays back down on the bed. And blindfolds himself.*) I'm ready Miss Crabtree! And I've been a very, very, bad boy!

(*From the bathroom enters SHEILA. SHE speaks in a baby voice.*)

SHEILA. Am I going to have to punish you, Wittle Cwaigy?

CRAIG. (*Baby talk.*) I think so.

(SHE starts tying his hands to the bed with scarves.)

CRAIG. Hey. Loretta ... What are you doing?

SHEILA. Ssh. Silence is Golden. (*SHE ties his hands to the bed posts.*)

CRAIG. (*Pleasantly surprised.*) Okay, Loretta!

SHEILA. You know better than to speak without raising your hand, Wittle Cwaigy.

CRAIG. But you're tying my hands down.

SHEILA. Don't make me get the ruler. Is that too tight?

CRAIG. (*Baby talk.*) No, Miss Crabtree.

SHEILA. Well, then ... (*Ties it tighter.*)

CRAIG. Ow

SHEILA. You're speaking again, Wittle Cwaigy. Am I going to have to make you stay after school and clean my erasers?

CRAIG. (*Enthusiastically, nodding in a naughty way.*) Mm-hm! God, Loretta, you are so full of little surprises.

SHEILA. You haven't seen anything yet, Devil Dog.

CRAIG. "Devil Dog?" God, Loretta, you haven't called me that since ... wait a minute. You've never called me that.

SHEILA. Sure I have, Devil Dog.

CRAIG. No you haven't.

SHEILA. Well, then. Who calls you that if I don't, Devil Dog? (*Playfully.*) One of your other girlfriends, maybe?

CRAIG. You know I don't have any other girlfriend. The only women in my life are you and my wi .... my ... my God!!! (*HE does a take with his blindfold on. HE then stares at her in horror.*)

SHEILA. What's wrong, Craig? Are you expecting a religious experience?

CRAIG. Sheila?!! Omigod, Sheila, is that you?

(*SHEILA takes off his mask. HE sees it is his wife. CRAIG gasps.*)

CRAIG. IT'S YOU!!

SHEILA. Hi, Craig. Remember me? (*HE screams.*)

SHEILA. Surprised?

CRAIG. I can explain.

SHEILA. I don't think so. (*From her suitcase SHEILA pulls out an electric drill.*)

CRAIG. Ah! Let's be reasonable ... Omigod. What are you going to do with that?

SHEILA. That depends on what you say in the next few minutes.

CRAIG. (*Petrified.*) Happy Birthday, Sheila.

(*SHE revs up the power drill.*)

CRAIG. (*Petrified.*) I love you, Sheila.

(*SHE revs up the power drill twice.*)

CRAIG. Okay. Okay. I had a meaningless little fling. I admit it. She works at the office. I'm sorry. I admit it. I lost my head. I'm sorry. I'll make it up to you. Look.

Look. My charge cards are in my jacket pocket. Take them. Go ahead. Take them. Go to Bloomingdales and spend like there's no tomorrow.

SHEILA. (*Revs up the power drill.*) You think you can buy me off with a green American Express card?

CRAIG. Stop it. Take this hat off my head. This is humiliating.

SHEILA. (*Laughs.*) Yes, I know.

CRAIG. How did you find me? It's my secretary, isn't it? That stupid secretary! This is her fault. She is fired. That stupid blabbermouth fathead secretary.

SHEILA. Your secretary didn't tell me. You did.

CRAIG. I did?

SHEILA. You don't really believe the wife is the last to know, do you?

CRAIG. I was kind of hoping.

SHEILA. You haven't fooled me these past few months, coming home late, locking yourself in the bathroom to talk on the phone with that towel stuffed under the door.

CRAIG. You've been spying on me! Oh, that is low. That is so low! This is so unlike you, Sheila. Okay. I'll forgive you this once. If you'll untie me, take this hat off my head and forgive me too.

SHEILA. Boy. You must think I'm really stupid. (*Revs drill.*)

CRAIG. No. Not at all. I ... I think you're the smartest woman alive. And the prettiest.

SHEILA. Oh, save it for your girlfriend. And just how long have you been making a fool out of me?

CRAIG. Not that long. Really. In fact, this is only the third time I was going to see her. I swear. It was nothing. A meaningless nothing. You're overreacting.

SHEILA. You're wearing a Cecil and Beanie hat, saddle shoes and you're tied to the bed. This is normal for you on a third date?

CRAIG. Okay. Fourth. This is the fourth date.

(SHE revs up the power drill.)

CRAIG. Okay. That's it. I'm through fooling around here. Untie me and take this hat off my head. Loretta's going to be here any minute.

SHEILA. I know. I want to get a good look at her.

CRAIG. No! I mean, Sheila, you don't want to do that.

SHEILA. Yes, I do. I want to see what she's got that's so special.

CRAIG. Nothing. She's got nothing. She's a loser.

SHEILA. A loser? Then why would you go with her?

CRAIG. I just felt so damn sorry for her. She's old. She's really old. She's so old that she uses a walker and sometimes a cane. And, you see … she'd never been with a man before. So I did this. As a good samaritan sort of gesture. It seemed like the Christian thing to do.

SHEILA. What a crock of shit.

CRAIG. Nice mouth, Sheila.

(There is a secret KNOCK at the door.)

CRAIG. Omigod. Go away!!

LORETTA. (*Off.*) Honey, it's me!

CRAIG. Oh, God.

LORETTA. (*Off.*) Let me in!

SHEILA. I better let her in.

CRAIG. Don't let her in.

SHEILA. I better let her in. We're on the twenty-third floor and since she's so old she's gonna want to sit down after climbing all the way up here with her little cane and walker.

CRAIG. No, don't, I ...

(SHE gags him with his bow tie and opens the door. LORETTA enters. SHE's a knockout. SHE sees the man tied to the bed and checks the door number.)

LORETTA. Oh, I'm sorry. I must have the wrong room.

SHEILA. Are you Loretta?

LORETTA. Yes.

SHEILA. I see that wrinkle cream is working.

LORETTA. What?

SHEILA. Come in, we were expecting you.

CRAIG. *(Spits out the gag.)* Run for your life! She's got a high-powered drill.

LORETTA. Omigod. Craig? Is that you?

CRAIG. *(Turning his face away and changing his voice.)* Uh ... no. I'm "Joe." Get out of our room. Don't listen to that woman with the drill. She's insane.

LORETTA. Craig, it is you. What's going on in here?

CRAIG. I'm "Joe."

LORETTA. *(To Sheila.)* Who are you?

SHEILA. I'm with him.

CRAIG. Oh God Oh God Oh God Oh God ...

LORETTA. What does she mean, "she's with you?"

CRAIG. *(As Joe.)* I don't know. She has a drill ...

SHEILA. I'm Sheila.

LORETTA. "Sheila?" You're Sheila? As in "Craig's wife, Sheila?"

SHEILA. Yes. Good old "Let's make a fool out of Sheila—Sheila." The same Sheila who sits at home alone eating Lean Cuisine while you grab each other under the table at Lutece. I'm the one you hang up on at two in the morning when you call our house to tell him you love him. I'm the one who takes care of the house and the shopping and the bills and all the other boring everyday crap so you two can roll around this hotel room every Monday night!

CRAIG. Hey. Don't think we don't appreciate it.

SHEILA. So, Loretta. Pleased to meet you. Now take your clothes off and put this on. (*SHEILA hands Loretta flimsy lingerie.*)

LORETTA. What? I'll do no such thing.

SHEILA. Really? That's funny after those polaroids I found of you in Craig's briefcase.

LORETTA. Omigod. Do something, Craig.

CRAIG. It's okay. I had an extra set of prints made.

LORETTA. Craig!

SHEILA. And now we're going to take a few more polaroids of you. But this time you can pose with my husband. And won't everyone at the office be surprised when I send them out as this year's Christmas card. Oh, when I get through humiliating you two you'll be lucky to get jobs scraping birdshit off a 747.

LORETTA. (*Teary.*) Craig ... I don't understand ... You said your wife was a big fat lesbian with asthma who spent all her nights at home in an oxygen tent.

SHEILA. What?

CRAIG. I never said that. What a liar.

LORETTA. Yes, you did.

CRAIG. She's insane, Sheila. The woman will say anything to get you mad at me.

SHEILA. That's an awfully elaborate lie for someone you've only dated three or four times, Craig.

LORETTA. Three or four times? Try three or four years.

SHEILA. Years? (*SHEILA starts beating him in the head with her suitcase.*) You miserable lying low-life ...

CRAIG. Ow! Stop it. Stop it, I'm telling you. You're making me mad, now.

LORETTA. Get your hands off him.

SHEILA. I will not.

LORETTA. Give me that. (*SHE takes the suitcase.*)

CRAIG. Thank you, Loretta.

LORETTA. If anyone's going to hit him, it's going to be me! (*SHE hits him too.*)

CRAIG. Ow! Ow! Cut it out, Loretta. Ow! Give that back to Sheila. You've got more upper body strength! Ow!

LORETTA. How could you? How could you? (*SHE pounds him with the suitcase in the lap.*)

CRAIG. Ow! I don't think I can anymore.

LORETTA. You are a liar.

SHEILA. He always was.

LORETTA. (*In tears, to Craig.*) And to think I believed you when you said even if your wife wasn't an asthmatic lesbian you could never sleep with her because she was wounded by shrapnel in a gangland drive-by shooting!

SHEILA. You believed that?

LORETTA. Yes. He even showed me fake photographs of you in your wheelchair.

SHEILA. Is that why you took those pictures of my Aunt Lois in the nursing home?

CRAIG. What are you complaining about? At least the flashbulbs kept her awake.

LORETTA. This means everything we had together was a lie. I bet the diamonds you gave me were fakes too.

SHEILA. Diamonds? He gave you diamonds?

LORETTA. These earrings and this bracelet.

SHEILA. For our anniversary I got a weed whacker. Wait a minute. Those are my earrings. That's my bracelet.

CRAIG. What an amazing coincidence.

SHEILA. He said we got "robbed" last summer while I was visiting my mother ... and ... you gave her my jewelry?

CRAIG. The insurance company paid us for them. And you hardly ever wore them ... And ... (*To Loretta.*) Thief! Thief! It was Loretta who robbed our house! Thank God I finally caught her after all these years.

SHEILA. Will you shut up?

LORETTA. You gave me used jewelry?

CRAIG. There is a recession on, if anyone cares to look around. You think it's easy pleasing two women?

SHEILA. You didn't.

LORETTA. At all.

CRAIG. Oh, sure. Nice. Go ahead. Mock my manhood now.

SHEILA. You've made a mockery of our entire marriage.

LORETTA. She's right. And I hate you for making me a part of all this. (*To Sheila, in tears.*) I'm sorry for any pain I caused for you, Sheila. I feel so guilty now about all the times he lied to you. Like the Christmas he said he had to spend the weekend in the office shredding secret documents because we were being audited by the IRS, he was really skiing with me in Vermont.

CRAIG. Oh, I was not! Like I even ski.

LORETTA. And those conventions he said he was at in Chicago, we were really off in the Poconos sitting in heart-shaped bathtubs. Oh, God, I'm so ashamed.

CRAIG. She makes it sound so glamorous. The towels were very thin. The rooms had that awful shag carpeting, and don't even get me started on the size of the food portions.

SHEILA. Now, now, Loretta. Calm down. This isn't all your fault. And I can see that now. I mean, how can I blame you? He told you I was a big fat lesbian.

CRAIG. Hey, you were a little heavier when I first met her.

(SHEILA slugs him with the suitcase. LORETTA sits on the bed.)

LORETTA. Sheila, you have to believe me. I would never sleep with a man whose wife wasn't a bedridden asthmatic imbedded with shrapnel.

SHEILA. *(Sitting opposite Loretta.)* I can tell that about you.

LORETTA. I want to kill you, Craig.

SHEILA. I know you do. So do I.

LORETTA. No one could blame us.

SHEILA. And no one would have to find out. They wouldn't find him until the morning when the housekeeper comes by.

LORETTA. That's right. And he's already tied up. He wouldn't even be able to struggle.

SHEILA. And so what if he did? A lot of people suffocate in rough sex situations. I saw that on "Geraldo" last week.

LORETTA. Oh, I taped that one. I haven't watched it yet.

CRAIG. Okay. That's enough now.

SHEILA. This could be really good. He is heavily insured anyway.

LORETTA. And I could move into his job at work so easily. And it pays $20,000 more a year.

CRAIG. Okay, girls ...

SHEILA. And we could split his credit cards. Mastercard for me, AMX for you.

LORETTA. (*Getting cozier on the bed.*) Could I have his BMW?

SHEILA. (*Settling in as well.*) Oh, sure. I'd want the Jag anyway.

LORETTA. Great.

CRAIG. All right. Fine. Very funny. Ha ha. Joke's over.

LORETTA. We'd be set for life.

CRAIG. That certainly was a good laugh at my expense. But "joke's over."

SHEILA. It would be so easy. We can even suffocate him with the dry cleaning bags I have down in the car.

CRAIG. Knock it off, Sheila.

LORETTA. And then we could use your drill to ruin any chance of identifying him by dental records.

SHEILA. That's right. And to throw the cops off the track, we can plant a love letter from his jealous lover, "Herman."

(THEY laugh.)

CRAIG. Okay. See this? See how we're all getting along now? Isn't this nice? And ... hey, since we already have the room, think of the possibilities ...

(SHEILA and LORETTA look at him in disgust.
LORETTA goes to the desk. SHEILA gets the drill.
The LIGHTS start to fade.)

SHEILA. *(Dictating.)* "My dearest, Craig. I've missed your touch. Your eyes. Your smell."
CRAIG. What are you doing?
LORETTA. "Your rough manly skin."
CRAIG. Loretta?
SHEILA. "Your Buster Brown pants."
CRAIG. Sheila?
SHEILA. "The way you scream and struggle every time we make love with our dry cleaning bags."
CRAIG. Girls? Girls? Oh, Girls ...

BLACKOUT

(We hear a DRILL.)

SCENE 3
"The Final Exit"

*All mimed to a Count Basie-like MUSICAL
SELECTION.*

CARL walks into room with a gift-wrapped package
and a briefcase. HE throws the gift and the briefcase on bed.

HE pops the briefcase open.

HE takes a framed picture of MELISSA out, kisses it
tearfully and sets it down on the desk. HE waves goodbye
to it.

HE walks away, taking a pen and hotel notepad with
him.

HE waves goodbye to MELISSA and starts writing a
"goodbye" letter.

HE puts the pen away, folds the paper and cuts his
finger.

HE sets note down by MELISSA's picture, goes to
gift-wrapped package on the bed and unwraps it. It is a
rifle.

CARL waves goodbye to MELISSA and tries killing
himself by shooting himself in the head various ways but
the rifle is too long for him to grip it and kill himself. HE
sets it on the floor, resting the barrel on his forehead. HE
reaches for the trigger. His arms are too short. HE drops
the rifle on his foot.

HE gets an idea and pulls an armchair over to the front
door and sets the rifle upside down on it facing the TV SL.
HE goes and sets the other chair in firing range.

HE picks up the phone and calls downstairs to get some
ice. HE hangs up the phone on his hand.

CARL lines up the rifle at the other chair. Goes and sits in it, and laughs to himself.

HE takes string out of his pocket and ties it from the trigger to the door knob.

HE goes and sits in his chair. HE cries to the picture, waving and kissing her goodbye. Crossing himself. Holding his ears, waiting for the explosion.

(SFX: KNOCK at the door.)

CARL mimes "Come in." "I said come in, come in." "Will you open the door now?" HE realizes the door is locked.

HE tiptoes to the door and opens it, then tiptoes back to his chair miming "Wait a minute. Don't open the door yet."

Finally seated, HE crosses himself and yells "Come in." "I said will you come in now?" He braces himself and the door opens. Into the room. The BELLBOY enters with ice.

CARL is shattered. His plan backfired. The BELLBOY asks where CARL wants his ice, and CARL yells to put it on the table SL. As he does, CARL inspects what went wrong at the front door. Disgusted with himself, CARL slams the door and the rifle goes off killing the BELLBOY.

Oblivious to the plight of the bellhop, CARL gets another idea and takes a knife to slash his wrists. HE cuts and cuts but nothing happens. HE checks for blood. Nothing.

HE cuts and cuts again, just as a bath-robed MAN and his WIFE from the adjoining room enter. CARL throws the knife away. The MAN is stabbed by the knife CARL discards.

CARL gets another idea and exits to the bathroom.

As the stabbed MAN dies, HE pulls the knife out of his back and accidentally stabs his wife as HE pulls HER down to the floor with him.

CARL enters from the bathroom with a glass of water and a pail. HE pours the water into it, takes a blowdryer from his bag and jumps in, dropping the blowdryer. Nothing happens.

CARL realizes the blowdryer isn't plugged in. HE gets out, plugs it in under the bed, and jumps back in. Nothing happens.

HE gets another idea. From his briefcase HE takes out dynamite sticks. HE goes to light them and realizes he doesn't have any matches.

As CARL turns upstage, a housecleaning MAID enters with towels. SHE sees the dead man and tries to revive him with water from the basin.

As SHE goes to reach, CARL checks the night stand for matches, but turns on the wall switch by the bed first. The night table LAMPS come on and the MAID is fried. CARL takes matches out from the night stand and lights the dynamite.

HE waits for it to blow. HE holds his ears and watches his watch. From the front door enters MELISSA. There has been a terrible misunderstanding. SHE wants him back. "Do you mean it?" "Yes I do. I feel so foolish I came here to kill myself." "How terrible." "Yes, I was going to blow my brains out, and slash my wrists and blow myself up."

CARL realizes he has to blow out the dynamite. HE does. THEY are both relieved. HE tosses the dynamite back into his briefcase.

THEY go to kiss.

The ROOM BLOWS UP. The ceiling caves in ... plaster and stuff. A DEAD BODY from the room upstairs.

CURTAIN

THE END

COSTUME PLOT

ACT I

<u>Scene 1</u>
CARL — Varsity jacket, dress shirt, slacks, black oxford shoes, white socks, glasses, watch cap (one set in pocket of jacket)
MELISSA — Cat suit, colorful blazer w/zipper, high heels
KEN — Business suit, dress shirt, tie, t-shirt boxer shorts, dress socks w/garters

<u>Scene 2</u>
JACK — Boxer shorts
ANNIE — Man's white shirt

<u>Scene 3</u>
ERIKKA — Black corset, black print dressing gown, black high heels, fish net stockings, viking helmet with horns
BELLHOP — Red bellhop jacket and cap, break-a-way black trousers, black t-shirt, boxer shorts, black socks, black shoes, fur vest, viking helmet with horns, red beard (hook-on type)
CUBBY — Hawaiian shirt, khaki pants, sneakers, gold chain & pinky ring
LYLE — Oversize fur vest, sword belt, fur boots, viking helmet with horns, shorts

<u>ACT</u> II

<u>Scene</u> 1
CLAUDIA — Lavender taffeta bridesmaid gown with full skirt and very large puffed sleeves, large lavender hairbow, dyed-to-match shoes
WALTER — Formal shirt, bow tie, boxer shorts, tuxedo pants (attached to Claudia's gown)
MRS. KIRSCHENBAUM — Lavender beaded chiffon mother-of-the-bride dress, silver shoes and bag, large corsage, pearl necklace, rhinestone earrings
RABBI HUCKELMAN — Poorly fitting dark suit, dress shirt, stained tie, prayer shawl, yarmulke
WENDY — Wedding gown with large expandable bustle and train, tuxedo pants attached to front of shirt, large bouquet, veil
GLENN — Formal shirt, bow tie, boxer shorts, black socks, tuxedo jacket

<u>Scene</u> 2
CRAIG — Business suit, dress shirt, tie, slip on shoes, t-shirt, boxer shorts, beanie w/propeller, saddle shoes
SHEILA — Fitted suit, high heels, wig
LORETTA — Suit

<u>Scene</u> 3
CARL — Same as Act I - Scene 1
MELISSA — Same as Act I - Scene 1
BELLHOP — Red bellhop jacket and cap, black trousers, black t-shirt
MAID — Black and white maid uniform, cap and apron, black high heels
MAN NEXT DOOR — Pajamas, bathrobe, slippers
WOMAN NEXT DOOR — Pajamas, bathrobe, slippers

PROPERTY LIST

ACT I

Scene 1
Champagne bottle, ice bucket, 2 champagne classes, telephone, TV remote control, wool ski hat

Scene 2
no props

Scene 3
2 quarters, 2 negligees, ice bucket with ice, 2 glasses, vodka, video camera, tripod, video tapes, desk lamp, room service menu, viking helmet, fur toga, script, red beard, ax, 2 five dollar bills, pad and pen

ACT II

Scene 1
Shaving kit, electric razor, marriage license, bridesmaid-dress-pants-stuck-ensemble, bridal bouquet, corsage, black pants

Scene 2
Champagne, 2 champagne glasses, note, eye glasses, beanie with helicopter top, big bow tie, saddle shoes, blind fold, 2 scarves, suitcase, credit cards, diamond earrings and bracelet, electric drill, flimsy lingerie, note pad & pen

Scene 3
Briefcase, large suitcase, letter, telephone, photo in frame, rifle, string, vase of flowers & water, ice bucket and tray,

bendable knife, blow dryer, sharp knife, stick of dynamite, matches, hat, magazine, Gideon Bible

Other Publications For Your Interest

DOCTOR DEATH. (All Groups.) Thriller-Farce. Mark Chandler. 3m., 9f. (can also be 4m, 8f. or 5m., 7f., via two male or female roles) That pixilated playwright of merry murder is at it again: The author of the marvelous *I Shot My Rich Aunt* takes us this time to the French Riviera, on a pleasure yacht just off Cap d'Antibes, where the happy guests of a mysterious host discover they're all marked for a madman's murderous vengeance. Their first clue that this will be less than a pleasant outing arrives in a deck of Old Maid cards, in which each is named—and rather nastily described. And with this clue comes the horrifying realization that one of them is a cruel and calculating killer. But which one? Can the malevolent mastermind be lovely Linda Luscious, handsome Victor Valor, bartender Margarita Martini, steward Queenie Quill, TV hostess Wendy Windy, shy secretary Portia Peck, sleazy Ritchy Raunchy, private-eye Harry Hulk, math-expert Sibyl Service, wrestler Minnie Mountain, actress Fanny Flop, or aerobics advocate Jillian Jogger? They'd better find out soon, because just after they realize that none of them can swim a stroke, they learn that the yacht is slowly sinking! (And in shark-filled waters, to boot!) Can they unmask the fiend in their midst? Can they figure out how to get off the doomed ship without drowning—or worse—in the process? Thrill follows chill in this madcap melodrama of hideous revenge—and there are so many gut-busting laughs along the way that you'll lose count! We promise you, this is a highly unusual variation on the trapped-by-a killer genre. The setting, the characters, and the convoluted plot are all superbly fascinating—and absolutely hilarious. A wonderfully zany evening of fun!   **#674**

I SHOT MY RICH AUNT. (All Groups.) Comedy. Mark Chandler. 4m., 5f. This rollicking romp through the British aristocracy's environs is a melange of off-the-wall farce and near-murder mystery. Every role is a gem and a delight for the performers. Lady Valonia Wendrew is having a number of people come to weekend at her stately manor (a former castle with a weird history) on the occasion of her nephew Dustin's announcement of his engagement to Judy Blake. Unluckily, Dustin's former flame Vivian Rexford has arrived to find out why Dustin dumped her two months previously, and Judy's brother Bingo Blake lets Dustin talk him into going outside to shoot at some starlings, and Lord Henry Mayhew, the family solicitor, is coming to change Valonia's will *out* of Dustin's favor, and Judy's school chum Gwendolyn Natterly is coming to meet—and ensnare—Dustin's cousin Nigel, a humble curate who thinks he's only there to meet Dustin's fiancee, and during the starling-shoot a stray bullet enters the library, and Dustin enters to find Valonia with a small hole in her blouse surrounded by oozing warm red liquid, and by the time he's run and gotten Bingo to come in and help him know what to do, the aunt's body has vanished and Eloise the maid is suspected to Know All and is planning to blackmail Dustin and meantime the picketing cooks' and maidservants' unions have raised the estate's drawbridge, thus entrapping everyone as night falls, and then Henry's wife thinks he's having an affair with Gwendolyn and she arrives with horsewhip in hand on the incoming fire engine (did we tell you the place is on fire?) You're going to be sore from the endless belly-laughs, all the way to the utterly insane finale!   **#11103**

WHAT THE BELLHOP SAW
(Little Theatre)
(FARCE)

by Wm. Van Zandt and Jane Milmore

8 male, 4 female

The play starts with a rather nice fellow checking into a $400.00 suite in "New York City's finest hotel". From there it snowballs into a fabulous nightmare involving a Salman Rushdie-type author, an Iranian Terrorist, a monstrous shrew-like woman, a conniving bellboy, a monumentally incompetent F.B.I. man, a nubile celebrity-mad maid, a dim-witted secretary, and a cute little pigtailed girl. All the while, gag lines are popping at Orville Redenbacher speed. Everything happens at pretty much whirlwind velocity. This latest farce by Van Zandt and Milmore combines topical humor with the traditional antics of farce: doors slamming, characters careening and confusion reigning supreme. A wildly funny farce! An excellent piece of workmanship by our two authors who take pride in the old-fashioned craft of comedy writing. #25062

THE SENATOR WORE PANTYHOSE
(Little Theatre)
(COMEDY)

by Wm. Van Zandt and Jane Milmore

7 male, 3 female

If you're tired of political and religious scandals, this is your greatest revenge! Van Zandt & Milmore's latest comedy revolves around the failing Presidential campaign of "Honest" Gabby Sandalson, a regular guy whose integrity has all but crippled his bid for the White House. Desparate for votes, his sleazeball campaign manager trumps up an implausible sex scandal which accidentally backfires on PMS Club leader Reverend Johnny and his makeup-faced wife Honey Pie; an opportunistic innkeeper with a penchant for antique food; the town's wayward single girl; two escaped convicts looking for stolen loot; and newscaster Don Bother. "A guaranteed hit!" (Asbury Park Press) "The characters swap beds, identities and jabs in what may be a flawless sex farce." (The Register). #21084

MIXED FEELINGS
(Little Theatre—Comedy)

Donald Churchill
m., 2 f., Int.

This is a riotous comedy about divorce, that ubiquitous, peculiar institution which so shapes practically everyone's life. Arthur and Norma, ex-spouses, live in separate apartments in the same building. Norma has second thoughts about her on-going affair with Arthur's best-friend; while Arthur isn't so sure he wants to continue *his* dalliance with Sonia, wife of a manufacturer with amusingly kinky sexual tastes (Dennis—the manufacturer—doesn't mind that his wife is having an affair; just so long as she continues to provide him with titillating accounts of it while he is dressed as a lady traffic cop). Most of Sonia's accounts are pure fiction, which seems to keep Dennis happy. Comic sparks are ignited into full-fledged farcical flames in the second act, when Dennis arrives in Arthur's flat for lessons in love from the legendary Arthur! "Riotous! A domestic laught romp! A super play. You'll laugh all the way home, I promise you.'—Eastbourne News. "Very funny ... a Churchill comedy that most people will thoroughly enjoy."—The Stage. Restricted New York City.

THE DECORATOR
(Little Theatre/Comedy)

Donald Churchill
m., 2 f., Int.

Much to her surprise, Marcia returns home to find that her flat has not been painted, as she arranged. In fact, the job hasn't even been started yet. There on the premises is the housepainter who is filling in for his ill colleague. As he begins work, there is a surprise visitor--the wife of the man with whom Marcia is having an affair, who has come to confront her nemesis and to exact her revenge by informing Marcia's husband of his wife's infidelity. Marcia is at her wit's end about what to do, until she gets a brilliant idea. It seems the housepainter is a part-time professional actor. Marcia hires him to impersonate her husband, Reggie, at the big confrontation later that day, when the wronged wife plans to return and spill the beans. Hilarity is piled upon hilarity as the housepainter, who takes his acting *very* seriously, portrays the absent Reggie. The wronged wife decides that the best way to get back at Marcia would be to sleep with her "husband" (the house painter), which is an ecstatic experience for them both. When Marcia learns that the housepainter/actor/husband has slept with her rival, she demands to have the opportunity to show the housepainter what *really* good sex is. "This has been the most amazing day of my life", says the sturdy painter, as Marcia leads him into her bedroom. "Irresistible."—London Daily Telegraph.